SPECIAL TIMES

A journey through life in
Christianity

Catherine House

Contents

Published by A & C Black
Publishers Limited
36 Soho Square
London W1D 3QY
www.acblack.com

ISBN 978-1-4081-2967-8

Copyright © A & C Black Publishers
Limited 2010

Series concept: Suma Din
Series consultant: Lynne Broadbent
Created by Bookwork Ltd, Stroud, UK

A CIP catalogue record for this book is
available from the British Library.

A & C Black uses paper produced with
elemental chlorine-free pulp, harvested
from managed sustainable forests. It
is natural, renewable and recyclable.
The logging and manufacturing process
conform to the environmental regulations
of the country of origin.

Printed in China by Leo Paper Products

All the internet addresses given in this
book were correct at the time of going to
press. The author and publishers regret
any inconvenience caused if addresses
have changed or sites have ceased to
exist, but can accept no responsibility for
any such changes.

4 How to use this book
An explanation of all the different features you will
find in this book.

6 A special gift from God
A birth in a Christian family is a very special time.
Christians believe that a baby is a gift from God.

8 Welcoming a new baby
Many Christians have a special service to welcome
a baby into the worldwide Christian family.

10 Learning how to be a Christian
As Christian children grow up they learn about
their religion and how to live a Christian life.

12 Receiving Holy Communion
Many Christians remember Jesus and his death in
a special service every week.

14 Growing up as a Christian
When young Christians understand the promises
they are making to God, they can decide to show
other people they want to live as Jesus taught.

16 Committing to Christian beliefs
The confirmation service is a time of celebration,
when people confirm they belong to God's family.

18 How to make a difference
As Christians grow up, they can put their beliefs
into practice through helping other people.

20 Choosing to be baptised

Some people are baptised and join the Christian community when they are older. They have a special service to celebrate their new Christian life.

22 Leading a Christian life

Being a Christian means more than just going to church or helping others. Many Christians believe it is about having a close relationship with God.

24 Loving others and marriage

Loving others is one of the most important parts of living a Christian life. One way that Christians show this love is through marriage.

26 The end of our life on Earth

Christians believe in life after death. They are not afraid of death because they believe that they will go to a better life with God.

28 When someone we love dies

It is a sad time when someone dies, but Christians try to remember happy times with that person. They thank God for the gift of that person's life.

30 Glossary and more information

An explanation of all the **bold** words in this book, and some ideas on where to find out more about Christianity.

32 Index

Use this to find topics in the book that interest you.

6 Baby Jesus, God's gift to the world

12 Holy Communion

24 Exchanging rings as a promise of love

How to use this book

People who follow the Christian religion are known as **Christians**. This book tells you what it is like to be Christian and about the special times, customs and beliefs of Christians.

Finding your way

The pages in this book have been carefully planned to make it easy for you to find out about Christianity. Here are two examples with explanations about the different features. Look at the Contents pages too, to read about each section.

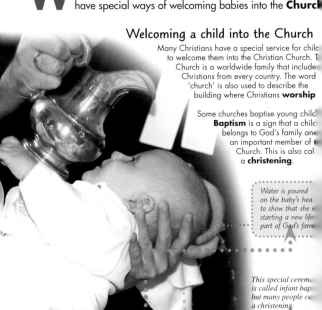

8   Birth

Welcoming a new baby

Welcoming a baby is very important. It makes them part of the worldwide Christian family. Christian communities have special ways of welcoming babies into the **Church**.

Welcoming a child into the Church

Many Christians have a special service for child to welcome them into the Christian Church. T Church is a worldwide family that includes Christians from every country. The word 'church' is also used to describe the building where Christians **worship**.

Some churches baptise young child **Baptism** is a sign that a chil belongs to God's family an an important member of Church. This is also cal a **christening**.

Water is poured on the baby's hea to show that she starting a new life part of God's fam

This special cerem is called infant bap but many people c a christening.

Comments give additional information about something specific in a picture.

Captions give a short description of a picture.

Bold words in the text are explained more fully in the glossary on page 30.

Boxed text gives extra information about a subject on the page.

Over to you... asks the reader to think more about their own customs and beliefs and how they compare to Christian beliefs.

Birth

A warm welcome

When a baby is born into a Christian family in Eritrea, Africa, the women give a long, loud call to let people know about the birth. A small child goes to every house in the village to share the news. Family and friends gather to welcome the new baby into the community. They bring a gift of enjera (a pancake-like bread) and thank God for the safe birth of the child.

...ervice of dedication

...me Christians, such as ...ptists, do not baptise very ...ng children. They believe ...t children should be able ...decide for themselves ...ether to become Christians ...not when they are older. ...ead, they have a service of ...dication. This means that ...parents promise to raise ...r baby in a way that will ...se God, until the child ...d enough to make the ...sion for themselves.

This is the baptis... service of a youn... girl in Tanzania, Africa. Her famil... stands with her as she joins the Christian Church...

Isabel is 7 years old. She lives in the UK. She has just been to her little brother's christening.

...When my baby brother was christened, I went out to the ...ront of the church. I was nervous because there were so ...many people. I stood with my family as the **vicar** baptised ...my brother. I didn't understand everything the vicar did, but ...knew it was a very special time. Then we had a party in ...ur garden. Our family came and then our friends.

Case studies give a Christian person's own experience of a custom described in the section.

2A Marriage   **Marriage 2B**

Loving others and marriage

L oving others is a major part of living a Christian life. One way of showing this love is by getting married. In the Bible, the relationship of a husband and wife is a very important one.

The wedding ceremony

The Christian wedding ceremony is a celebration of thanks to God for the gift of marriage. Family and friends all take part in the ceremony because it is a sign of God's love for everyone.

The couple make promises in front of God. They give each other rings. Rings are unbroken with no end so they are used as symbols that a couple's love will never end.

At the end of the ceremony, the minister asks God to bless the couple in their new life together.

Jesus taught his followers that the most important thing in life was to love God and each other.

My command is this: Love each other as I have loved you.

Exchanging rings shows that the two people belong to each other.

Wedding rings remind the couple of the promises they have made to each other.

Over to you...
• Where do people in your community get married? Why do people choose different places?
• What do the bride and groom promise during a Christian marriage ceremony?

Celibacy

Not every Christian gets married. Jesus taught that some people will choose not to get married because they want to give their whole life to loving God and helping others. This is called celibacy. Today, Catholic priests, monks and nuns make a promise not to get married, devoting their life to God.

The bride and groom stand beside each other at the altar.

What is love like?

Christians believe that they should love other people in the same way as Jesus did. The Bible teaches that this kind of love should be shown in many ways. A person should be kind, patient and forgiving. They should not be boastful or proud. They should not be rude to anyone or get angry with them easily. Love means thinking of others before yourself and protecting those that you love.

A wedding in church shows that God is part of the couple's life.

Quotes are taken from the Bible, the Christian holy book.

A special gift from God

The Virgin Mary was Jesus' mother. His birth is very special to Christians because he is God's own son.

Life is like a journey, and birth is the beginning. The birth of a child is always a time of wonder. Christians feel excited as a new gift from God comes into the world.

The gift of life

Christians (followers of Jesus) believe that a new life is a gift from God. They believe that everyone is special to God, so it is important to respect each other and the gift of life.

The most important birth for Christians is the birth of Jesus. The **Bible** (the Christian holy book) says that he was God's special gift to the world. Jesus' birth is celebrated at **Christmas**.

God's creations

Christians believe that God gives life to every baby. The Bible says that God creates each new person:

You are the one who put me together in my mother's body, and I praise you because of the wonderful way you created me.

Over to you...

● How do people celebrate birth in your community?

● How do Christians celebrate Jesus' birth?

● What are the things that make you special?

God's blessing

Christians celebrate the birth of a baby by thanking God. Some Christians want their new baby to be blessed. A **blessing** is a special **prayer** asking for God's help and protection.

The **minister** says these words:

"Heavenly father, we thank you for this birth;
Surround this baby with your blessing
That this child may know your love,
Be protected from evil
And know your goodness
all their days."

A baby is blessed by a minister. His parents want God to be part of his life from a young age.

The minister puts a hand on the baby's head to ask for God's blessing.

Welcoming a new baby

Welcoming a baby is very important. It makes them part of the worldwide Christian family. Christian communities have special ways of welcoming babies into the **Church**.

Welcoming a child into the Church

Many Christians have a special service for children to welcome them into the Christian Church. The Church is a worldwide family that includes Christians from every country. The word 'church' is also used to describe the building where Christians **worship**.

Some churches baptise young children. **Baptism** is a sign that a child belongs to God's family and is an important member of the Church. This is also called a **christening**.

> Water is poured on the baby's head to show that she is starting a new life as part of God's family.

This special ceremony is called infant baptism, but many people call it a christening.

A warm welcome

When a baby is born into a Christian family in Eritrea, Africa, the women give a long, loud call to let people know about the birth. A small child goes to every house in the village to share the news. Family and friends gather to welcome the new baby into the community. They bring a gift of enjera (a pancake-like bread) and thank God for the safe birth of the child.

Service of dedication

Some Christians, such as Baptists, do not baptise very young children. They believe that children should be able to decide for themselves whether to become Christians or not when they are older. Instead, they have a service of dedication. This means that the parents promise to raise their baby in a way that will please God, until the child is old enough to make the decision for themselves.

This is the baptism service of a young girl in Tanzania, Africa. Her family stands with her as she joins the Christian Church.

Isabel is 7 years old. She lives in the UK. She has just been to her little brother's christening.

When my baby brother was christened, I went out to the front of the church. I was nervous because there were so many people. I stood with my family as the **vicar** baptised my brother. I didn't understand everything the vicar did, but I knew it was a very special time. Then we had a party in our garden. Our family came and then our friends.

Learning how to be a Christian

As Christian children grow up, they learn about their religion at church, at home and sometimes at school. Christians teach children about Jesus' life and the things that he taught.

Learning from the Bible

There are lots of ways that children can learn about God. They learn from the Bible, through worship and also prayer. Many churches hold clubs or classes for children, where they learn about the stories in the Bible. Christians believe that these are a gift from God to help them live the right way, and that reading the Bible is an important way to find out about God. It is a very special book.

The Bible teaches that God is a loving God. Jesus taught that people should show love in their lives. He told his followers that the most important rules in life were to love God and to love other people.

These children are listening to Bible stories in their Sunday school in Ghana, Africa.

Learning through objects

Children can learn through pictures and objects. Different Christian families have different objects in their homes. Some families may have a **crucifix** (a cross showing Jesus' body), or a statue of Mary, the mother of Jesus. These objects help the family to think about Jesus when they are praying.

Over to you...

● Are there any religious pictures or symbols in your own home? Find out what they all mean.

● Do you know any Bible stories?

Learning at home

Christians believe that God can be worshipped everywhere, not just at church. Parents pray with their children before they go to bed so they know that God loves them. Families pray before they eat meals so that children learn to be thankful for all of God's gifts, such as the food they eat. Children also find out how to live as Christians and followers of Jesus by being part of a Christian community. They can learn from copying the way other people live.

A mother and daughter read the Bible together at bedtime.

Receiving Holy Communion

T he Bible says that before Jesus died, he shared a special meal with his **disciples** (followers, also known as apostles), called the Last Supper. As they ate and drank, Jesus told his disciples always to remember him in the same way.

Holy Communion

Many Christians remember Jesus and his death at a service every week. This service is called Mass, Holy **Communion**, Eucharist, the Lord's Supper or the breaking of bread. They eat a small piece of bread and sip some wine, as the disciples did at the Last Supper.

Why do Christians remember Jesus' death?

Christians believe that Jesus died to pay for their sins (the wrong things they do). During Communion they say sorry for their sins and thank God for his forgiveness. For many Christians, Communion is more than a time for remembering Jesus' death. They believe that Jesus' spirit is really with them.

The bread and wine are served in a special dish and chalice (cup).

Celebrating Holy Communion is like sharing a big, family meal.

> *Jesus broke the bread and handed it to his apostles.*
> *Then he said, "Eat this as a way of remembering me."*

First Communion

A child's first Communion is very special. In some Churches, small children can take Communion. Children who belong to the Catholic Church celebrate their first Communion when they are about eight years old. In some other Christian Churches, children take Communion only when they are teenagers or after they have been confirmed (see page 14). Different Churches obey Jesus' teaching in different ways.

Many Catholic children, like these in Gambia, Africa, wear special clothes to celebrate their first Communion.

Growing up as a Christian

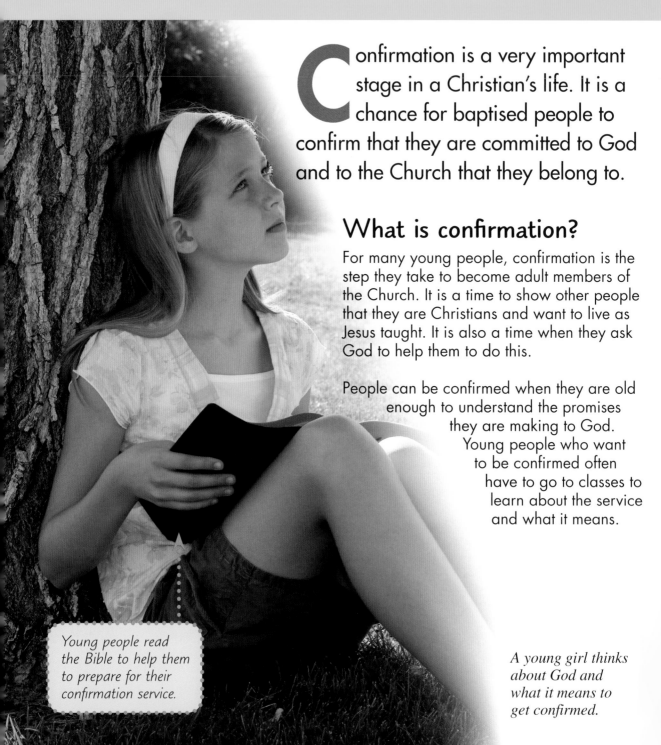

Confirmation is a very important stage in a Christian's life. It is a chance for baptised people to confirm that they are committed to God and to the Church that they belong to.

What is confirmation?

For many young people, confirmation is the step they take to become adult members of the Church. It is a time to show other people that they are Christians and want to live as Jesus taught. It is also a time when they ask God to help them to do this.

People can be confirmed when they are old enough to understand the promises they are making to God. Young people who want to be confirmed often have to go to classes to learn about the service and what it means.

Young people read the Bible to help them to prepare for their confirmation service.

A young girl thinks about God and what it means to get confirmed.

> *Peter and John then placed their hands on everyone who had faith in the Lord, and they were given the Holy Spirit.*

The Holy Spirit

The Holy Spirit is God's Spirit working in the world. Christians believe that the Holy Spirit is inside them, helps them live a Christian life and gives them a feeling of peace and joy. Another name given to the Holy Spirit is 'helper'.

A minister prays for a boy to be filled with God's Spirit.

Receiving the Holy Spirit

The Bible describes how the first Church leaders put their hands on Christians' heads and prayed that they would receive the **Holy Spirit**. Today, many Christian leaders follow their example when someone wants to confirm their **faith** in God. In some Churches, this happens at a confirmation service.

Luke is 12 years old. He lives in London. He has been preparing for his confirmation.

My confirmation class was like a discussion group. We learnt about the things that Christians believe and what it means to be a member of our Church. It was a chance to ask difficult questions about God and to find some answers. These discussions helped me to decide that I wanted to get confirmed. I feel this is the next step for me to take as a Christian.

Committing to Christian beliefs

Getting confirmed is a time of celebration. A person who is being confirmed is pleased that they are doing what God wants and is happy that they belong to God's family.

The confirmation service

People from different churches in an area join together for confirmation services. In many churches, a leader called a **bishop** leads the service. Family and friends join in. The bishop asks these questions:

- Have you been baptised?
- Are you ready to affirm your faith in Jesus Christ?
- Are you sorry for the wrong things you do?
- Do you come to Jesus as Lord and Saviour?

This girl is being confirmed by a priest in Hiroshima, Japan.

The bishop then puts his hands on the heads of the people to be confirmed and asks God for his Holy Spirit.

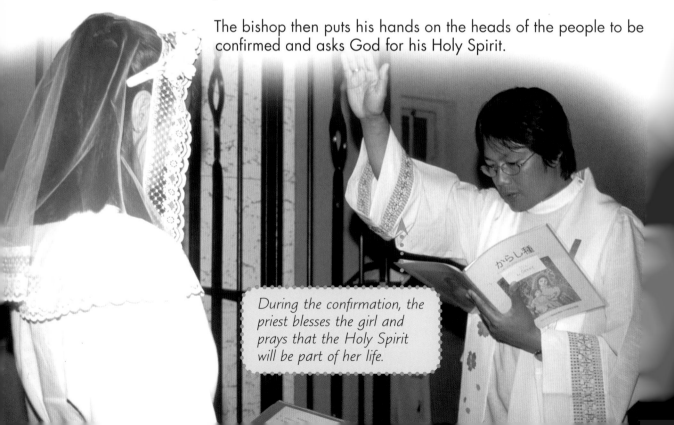

During the confirmation, the priest blesses the girl and prays that the Holy Spirit will be part of her life.

> *Confirm, O Lord, your servant with your Holy Spirit. Amen.*

Over to you...

● What groups do you belong to at school and in your community?

● How do you show your commitment to these groups?

Salvation Army officers wear a uniform to show other people who they are.

Other ways to show commitment

Not every Christian group has a service of confirmation. Young people show that they are committed to their Christian beliefs in lots of different ways.

Young people in the Salvation Army (a worldwide Christian Church) have a special ceremony in which they promise to obey the teachings of the Bible and the Salvation Army.

Other Christian groups practise believer's baptism. Young people and adults confirm their faith during a special service when they are totally covered with water (see page 20).

An Australian woman plays a tambourine in the Salvation Army. It is traditional for the Salvation Army to play music in the streets during parades, services and at Christmas.

How to make a difference

Growing up is exciting because you can take on more responsibility at school, at home and in your community. For young Christian people, it also means learning how to put their Christian beliefs into action, such as by helping others.

Young Christians

The Bible teaches Christians that Jesus loved God and other people. Christians try to show the same love in their own lives. They believe that people have different gifts and abilities, which can all be used to help people in the Church and in the community.

Young people have an important role in the Church. They take part in worship and help with church activities, such as playing in a music group or teaching younger children.

These children in India are praying for other people and for the world.

Simon is 18 years old. He is a volunteer for Christians in Sport.

Sport is my God-given passion. I try to play in a way that honours God, pray for my sporting friends and share my love for Jesus with others. Last summer, I **volunteered** to work with Christians in Sport and helped to run sporting activities for children. I love working with children. It's great to be able to help them and see them improving. And I can help them learn more about God as well as their sport.

> *Don't let anyone make fun of you, just because you are young. Set an example for other followers by what you say and do.*

Helping others

There are many ways that young people can make a difference in their families, schools and communities. Young Christian people believe that they should use their talents and abilities to help others. On these pages are examples of young people who are helping to make a difference. Such young people are setting a good example for other Christians.

Louise is 15. She helps to look after younger children during her church service.

Jama lives in Indonesia. After his island was hit by a tsunami (a huge wave), he worked with his church to help rebuild the destroyed houses in his village.

Choosing to be baptised

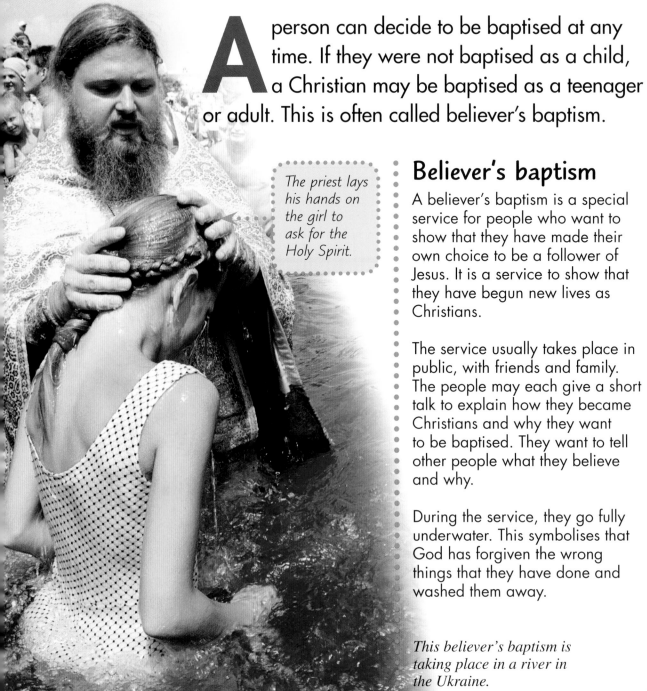

A person can decide to be baptised at any time. If they were not baptised as a child, a Christian may be baptised as a teenager or adult. This is often called believer's baptism.

The priest lays his hands on the girl to ask for the Holy Spirit.

Believer's baptism

A believer's baptism is a special service for people who want to show that they have made their own choice to be a follower of Jesus. It is a service to show that they have begun new lives as Christians.

The service usually takes place in public, with friends and family. The people may each give a short talk to explain how they became Christians and why they want to be baptised. They want to tell other people what they believe and why.

During the service, they go fully underwater. This symbolises that God has forgiven the wrong things that they have done and washed them away.

This believer's baptism is taking place in a river in the Ukraine.

The minister lowers the girl into the water, with one hand behind her and one in front.

The importance of baptism

When a baptised person comes out of the water, they are ready to live a new life as a follower of Jesus. This is only possible with the help of God's Holy Spirit. Baptism is important because Jesus told his followers to do this. He said:

> *Baptise them in the name of the Father, the Son and the Holy Spirit.*

A girl is baptised in a baptismal pool to receive the Holy Spirit. The dove (above) is a symbol of the Holy Spirit.

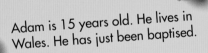

Adam is 15 years old. He lives in Wales. He has just been baptised.

I decided to be baptised when I felt it was the right time for me. I felt quite nervous before the service and was shaking when I spoke about my Christian beliefs in front of everyone. After I came out of the water, it was really wonderful. My whole family came with me to the service. Some of them were quite surprised. They hadn't realised how strongly I felt about my Christian beliefs.

Leading a Christian life

Many Christians believe that being a Christian is like a journey. Some start the journey as children when they are christened. Other people become Christians later in life. But whenever they make this decision, all Christians share similar beliefs.

What makes someone a Christian?

Most Christians believe that the Christian life is much more than doing good things, going to church and taking part in special services. For many, being a Christian is about having a **relationship** with God. They believe that Jesus is alive today and can be a very close friend.

Christians have a relationship with God by talking to Him through prayer.

Over to you...

● What things do Christians do to show what they believe?

● Why do you think Christians do all these things?

Do Christians have to go to church?

No. The first Christians did not have church buildings. However, most Christians today believe that it is important to be part of a group with other Christians, so they do go to church. This is because the Bible teaches that Christians should help each other and worship together. But some people are unable to get to church or prefer to worship with others at home.

These Christians are worshipping with others in a church. Christians usually go to church on Sunday.

What do Christians do?

*Christians believe that it is important to help people in need. Many are involved in projects all over the world, such as those that help the poor, sick or homeless. Christians often speak out for **justice** if they think someone is being treated unfairly. They tell others about Jesus and try to love God and other people, as Jesus taught. They show this love by being forgiving, by helping people and by living honestly.*

Loving others and marriage

Loving others is a major part of living a Christian life. One way of showing this love is by getting married. In the Bible, the relationship of a husband and wife is a very important one.

Exchanging rings shows that the two people belong to each other.

The wedding ceremony

The Christian wedding ceremony is a celebration of thanks to God for the gift of marriage. Family and friends all take part in the ceremony because it is a sign of God's love for everyone.

The couple make promises in front of God. They give each other rings. Rings are unbroken with no end so they are used as symbols that a couple's love will never end.

At the end of the ceremony, the minister asks God to bless the couple in their new life together.

Jesus taught his followers that the most important thing in life was to love God and each other.

My command is this:

Love each other as I have loved you.

Wedding rings remind the couple of the promises they have made to each other.

Over to you...

- Where do people in your community get married? Why do people choose different places?

- What do the bride and groom promise during a Christian marriage ceremony?

Celibacy

Not every Christian gets married. Jesus taught that some people will choose not to get married because they want to give their whole life to loving God and helping others. This is called celibacy. Today, Catholic priests, monks and nuns make a promise not to get married, devoting their life to God.

The bride and groom stand beside each other at the altar.

What is love like?

Christians believe that they should love other people in the same way as Jesus did. The Bible teaches that this kind of love should be shown in many ways. A person should be kind, patient and forgiving. They should not be boastful or proud. They should not be rude to anyone or get angry with them easily. Love means thinking of others before yourself and protecting those that you love.

A wedding in church shows that God is part of the couple's life.

The end of our life on Earth

This window is in St James Church in Delhi, India. It shows the Resurrection of Jesus.

Christians believe that death is not the end of life's journey. It is the door that leads to a better life with God. They believe that Christians will live with God for ever in a place of happiness where there is no illness or death.

Resurrection

Christians believe in life after death because Jesus died and came back to life. Christians call this the **Resurrection** and celebrate it at **Easter**. Jesus told his disciples not to be afraid of death because he would care for them and take them to God in **Heaven**. Many Christians believe in a final resurrection when God will bring everyone back to life. Jesus said:

Do not let your hearts be troubled. Trust in God; trust also in me.

Easter

Easter is an important festival for Christians. On Good Friday, they remember that Jesus died on the cross. On Easter Sunday, they celebrate the Resurrection of Jesus. Churches are filled with flowers and joyful hymns are sung. Some people decorate and eat eggs because eggs symbolise the Resurrection and the start of a new life.

Preparing for death

Christians believe that it is important to help people to prepare for death, just as Jesus cared for people who were sick and dying. Today, Christians follow his example by comforting and helping people facing this stage in life's journey.

Helen House hospice

Helen House was the first hospice (a place where very ill people are cared for) for children. It was founded by Sister Frances Dominica. Sister Frances Dominica is a Christian who has spent her life helping children and young people with serious illnesses.

Sister Frances Dominica

Garvan stayed at Helen House hospice. This is what he believed would happen when he died.

As I'm sitting here, I'm Garvan, right — but this isn't really me. My body is just a reflection. When I die, I will leave my body and that reflection will fade. But the real me won't die. My real self will leave my body and go up to God. At that moment, when I die, I believe Jesus will be standing beside me with his arms outstretched, ready to take me to his Father. Imagine the sheer excitement of meeting Him for the first time!

When someone we love dies

People celebrate the life of loved ones in different ways. Many Christians bury the body of people who have died. Some Christians ask to be buried in the ground when they die. Others choose to be turned into ashes at a **cremation**.

How do Christians feel at a funeral?

Christians feel many different things at a funeral. They are very sad because they have lost somebody they love. They are also thankful to God for the gift of that person's life and believe that there is another life after death. Christians believe that God brings comfort to people who are sad because of the death of a loved one.

'Fantasy coffins' of Ghana come in all shapes and sizes. This fish shape shows that the person was a fisherman.

In Ghana, a funeral is an important way for a whole community to celebrate a person's life. Some people choose a colourful **coffin** to honour the person. The shape of the coffin celebrates something about that person. A favourite shape for Christians is a Bible.

Graveyards

Christians believe they will live with God for ever after they have died. Church graveyards often have yew trees as symbols of everlasting life. This is because these trees do not lose their leaves in winter.

Over to you...

● What symbols are used at funeral services in different religions? What do they mean?

● How do people celebrate the life of people who have died in your community?

Lizzie is 15 years old. Her uncle has recently died.

I went to the cremation of my uncle. It was really hard and I cried through the service. Afterwards we went to a **memorial service** at his church. This was happier because they told funny stories about him and played a video showing parts of his life. My uncle had died from cancer and I was happy that he was no longer in pain.

Christians may have a cross on top of their grave to show that they believe in Jesus and his Resurrection.

Glossary and more information

baptism The ceremony performed to admit someone into the *Church*.

Bible The *Christian* holy book, consisting of the Old and New Testaments.

bishop A senior *minister* in charge of the *churches* in a particular area.

blessing A *prayer* asking for good things to happen to a person.

christening The *baptism* of a child, when he or she is also given a name.

Christian A follower of Jesus. Also, a word that describes things belonging to Christianity.

Christmas A festival celebrating the birth of Jesus.

Church The name given to a community who *worship* Jesus together. Also, a building where *Christians* worship.

coffin A box in which the body of a dead person is placed before burial.

Communion A *Christian service* that remembers Jesus' last meal with his *disciples*.

cremation A form of burial where the body is burnt until it turns to ash.

crucifix Model of a cross with Jesus on it. Jesus was nailed to a cross to die.

disciple A person who followed Jesus while he was alive and studied his teaching.

Easter A festival celebrating the life, death and *Resurrection* of Jesus.

faith Strong belief in a religion.

Heaven The place where God lives and where *Christians* go when they die.

Holy Spirit God's Spirit working in the world. *Christians* believe in one God as three persons: the Father, Son and Holy Spirit.

justice When someone is treated fairly.

memorial service A *service* to honour and remember a person who has died.

minister The name given to a person who works for and leads a *church*.

prayer A way of talking to God to ask Him for something or to thank Him.

relationship The way in which two or more people are connected with each other.

Resurrection When Jesus came back to life after he died on the cross.

service A ceremony when people meet to *worship* God together.

vicar The name given to some *Christian ministers*.

volunteer To work without payment.

worship To thank God for what He does and who He is.

Things to do

Ask your teacher to help you to organise a visit to a church in your community. Find out the meaning of the symbols and objects that you find in the church. Ask the minister or a member of the church to describe what happens in the church when people get married, baptised as a baby or adult and confirmed.

Tell the story of the birth of Jesus to some friends. Explain to them why the festival of Christmas is important to Christians.

Ask your teacher if you can invite someone from the local Christian community to talk to your class about the meaning of Easter.

In this book are some different examples of religious art, including stained-glass windows like the one on page 26. Design your own stained-glass window to illustrate a topic in this book.

More information

Find out more about Christianity on these websites.

Websites

For teachers
www.bbc.co.uk/schools/religion/ christianity
Pages from the BBC Schools website, giving an introduction to Christianity, Christian festivals and suggested class activities for Key Stages 1 and 2.
pof.reonline.org.uk/christianity.php
This website gives an explanation of some different Christian denominations and their practices.
www.cofe.anglican.org/lifeevents/ baptismconfirm/
These pages from the Anglican Church give further information about baptism and confirmation services.
www.baptist.org.uk/baptist_life/ believers_baptism.html
These pages from the Baptist Union give a fuller explanation of believer's baptism.

For children
www.request.org.uk
A child-friendly website that provides visual information, including video clips, about the beliefs and practices of different types of Christian groups.
www.globalgang.org
A fun Christian Aid website for primary schools, which encourages children to make a difference in the world. You will find everything here from games to information about things that are happening in the world today.

Index

AB
adults 14, 17, 20
altars 25
apostles 12, 13
ashes 28
Australia 17
babies 6–7, 8–9
baptisms 8–9, 14, 16, 17, 20–21
    believer's 17, 20–21
    infant 8–9
baptismal pools 21
Baptists 9
beliefs 6, 9, 10, 11, 12, 16–17, 18, 20, 21, 22–23, 25, 26, 27, 28, 29
believer's baptism 17, 20–21
Bible 6, 10, 11, 12, 14, 17, 18, 23, 24, 25, 28
Bible stories 10, 11
birth 6–9
bishops 16
blessings 7, 24
bread 12, 13
brides 25
burials 28

C
Catholics 13, 25
celebrations 6, 7, 12, 13, 16, 24, 26, 28
celibacy 25
ceremonies 8, 17, 24
chalices 12

children 10–11, 13, 19, 20, 27
christenings 8–9, 22
Christians in Sport 18
Christmas 6, 17
Churches 8, 9, 13, 14, 15, 18
    Catholic 13
churches 8, 9, 10, 16, 18, 19, 22, 23, 25, 27, 29
classes 10, 14, 15
clothes 13
coffins 28
    fantasy 28
Communion (see Holy Communion)
communities 8, 9, 11, 18, 19, 28
confirmation 13, 14–15, 16, 17
cremations 28–29
crosses 11, 27, 29
crucifixes 11

DE
death 12, 26–29,
dedication, services of 9
disciples 12, 26
Dominica, Sister Frances 27
doves 21
Easter 26, 27
eggs 27
Eritrea, Africa 9
Eucharist (see Holy Communion)
evil 7

FG
faith 15, 16, 17
families 8, 9, 11, 12, 16, 20, 21, 24,
fantasy coffins 28
festivals 27
fishermen 28
flowers 27
food 11
forgiveness 12, 23, 25
friends 9, 16, 20, 22, 24
funerals 28, 29
Gambia, Africa 13
Ghana, Africa 10, 28
gifts 6, 10, 11, 18, 24, 28
God 6, 7, 8, 9, 10, 11, 12–13, 14, 15, 16, 17, 18, 19, 20, 21, 22, 23, 24, 25, 26, 27, 28
Good Friday 27
graves 29
graveyards 28
grooms 25

HIJK
Heaven 26
Helen House 27
Holy Communion 12–13
Holy Spirit 15, 16, 17, 20, 21
homes 10, 11, 18, 23
homeless 23
hospices 27

husbands 24
hymns 27
illness 27
India 18
Indonesia 19
infant baptisms 8–9
Japan 16
Jesus 6, 10, 11, 12, 13, 16, 17, 18, 19, 20, 21, 22, 23, 25, 26, 27, 29
joy 15
justice 23

LMN
Last Supper 12
Lord's Supper (see Holy Communion)
love 7, 10, 11, 18, 24–25, 28
marriage 24–25
Mary 6, 11
Mass (see Holy Communion)
meals 11, 12
memorial services 29
ministers 7, 15
monks 25
music 17, 18
nuns 25

OPQ
parades 17
parents 7, 9, 11
peace 15
poor 23
prayers 7, 10, 11, 15, 18, 22
priests 16, 20, 25

RS
relationships 22, 24
responsibilities 18
Resurrection 26, 27, 29
rings 24
Salvation Army 17
schools 10, 18, 19
    Sunday 10
services 8, 9, 12, 14, 15, 16, 17, 19, 20, 21, 22, 29
    memorial 29
sick 23, 27
sins 12
Sunday 23, 27
Sunday school 10
symbols 11, 20, 21, 24, 28

TUV
Tanzania, Africa 9
teaching 18
teenagers 13, 20
Ukraine 20
vicars 9
villages 9, 19
Virgin Mary (see Mary)
volunteering 18

WXYZ
water 8, 17, 20, 21
weddings 24–25
wine 12
wives 24
worship 8, 10, 11, 18, 23
yew trees 28

Picture credits

The publisher would like to thank the following for their kind permission to reproduce their photographs:

Position key: c=centre; b=bottom; t=top; l=left; r=right

1c: Christine Osborne/World Religions Photo Library; 3 tr: Christine Osborne/World Religions Photo Library; 3cr: Christine Osborne/World Religions Photo Library; 3br: Daniel Sagatowski/World Religions Photo Library; 5bl: Galina Barskaya/shutterstock; 6cl: Roca/shutterstock; 7bc: Vadim Kzlovsky/shutterstock; 8bl: Martin Kucera/shutterstock; 9bl: Galina Barskaya/ shutterstock; 9cr: Christine Osborne/World Religions Photo Library; 10bc: Christine Osborne/World Religions Photo Library; 11tr: Wheatley/shutterstock; 11c: Lisa F Young/shutterstock; 12bl: Wojtek Kryczka/istockphoto; 12bl: Wojtek Kryczka/istockphoto; 12br: Christine Osborne/World Religions Photo Library; 13c: Christine Osborne/World Religions Photo Library; 14cl: Tera Flake/istockphoto; 15bl: Photomynd/ shutterstock; 15tr: Paul Gapper/World Religions Photo Library; 16bc: Angeles Marin/World Religions Photo Library; 17c: Tim Gurney/World Religions Photo Library; 18bl: Hannah Roche; 18cl: BMS World Mission;19tr: Andrew House; 19bc: BMS World Mission; 20bl: Roman Kravchenko/World Religions Photo Library; 21tr: Balakirev Vladmir/shutterstock; 21bl: Jaimie Duplass/shutterstock; 21tc: Paul Gapper/ World Religions Photo Library; 22bc: Christine Osborne/World Religions Photo Library; 23bl: Lisa F Young/shutterstock; 23tc: Tim Gurney/World Religions Photo Library; 24cl: Wai Chan/shutterstock; 24bc: KonceptuS/shutterstock; 25cr: istockphoto; 26cl: Julian Worker/World Religions Photo Library; 27bl: Fidelis Byrne; 27cr: Steve Wheeler; 27tc: Chinch Gryniewicz, World Religions Photo Library; 28bl: Wolfgang Rattay/ Reuters/Corbis; 29c: Nicole S Young/istockphoto; 29c: Monkey Business Images/shutterstock

Cover photograph © Enigma/Alamy